HOMES

A Look at THEN and NOW

PERCY LEED

GRL Consultant, Diane Craig, Certified Literacy Specialist

Lerner Publications ◆ Minneapolis

Educator Toolbox

Reading books is a great way for kids to express what they're interested in. Before reading this title, ask the reader these questions:

> What do you think this book is about? Look at the cover for clues.
>
> What do you already know about homes in the past?
>
> What do you want to learn about homes in the past?

Let's Read Together

Encourage the reader to use the pictures to understand the text.

Point out when the reader successfully sounds out a word.

Praise the reader for recognizing sight words such as *in* and *or*.

TABLE OF CONTENTS

Homes Then and Now 4

You Connect! 21
Social and Emotional Snapshot 22
Photo Glossary .23
Learn More 23
Index. 24

Homes Then and Now

People have lived in homes for many years.

THEN
Families used oil lamps.

NOW
We use electric lamps.

THEN

Families kept food in big boxes. Ice kept food cold.

NOW

We use electric fridges.

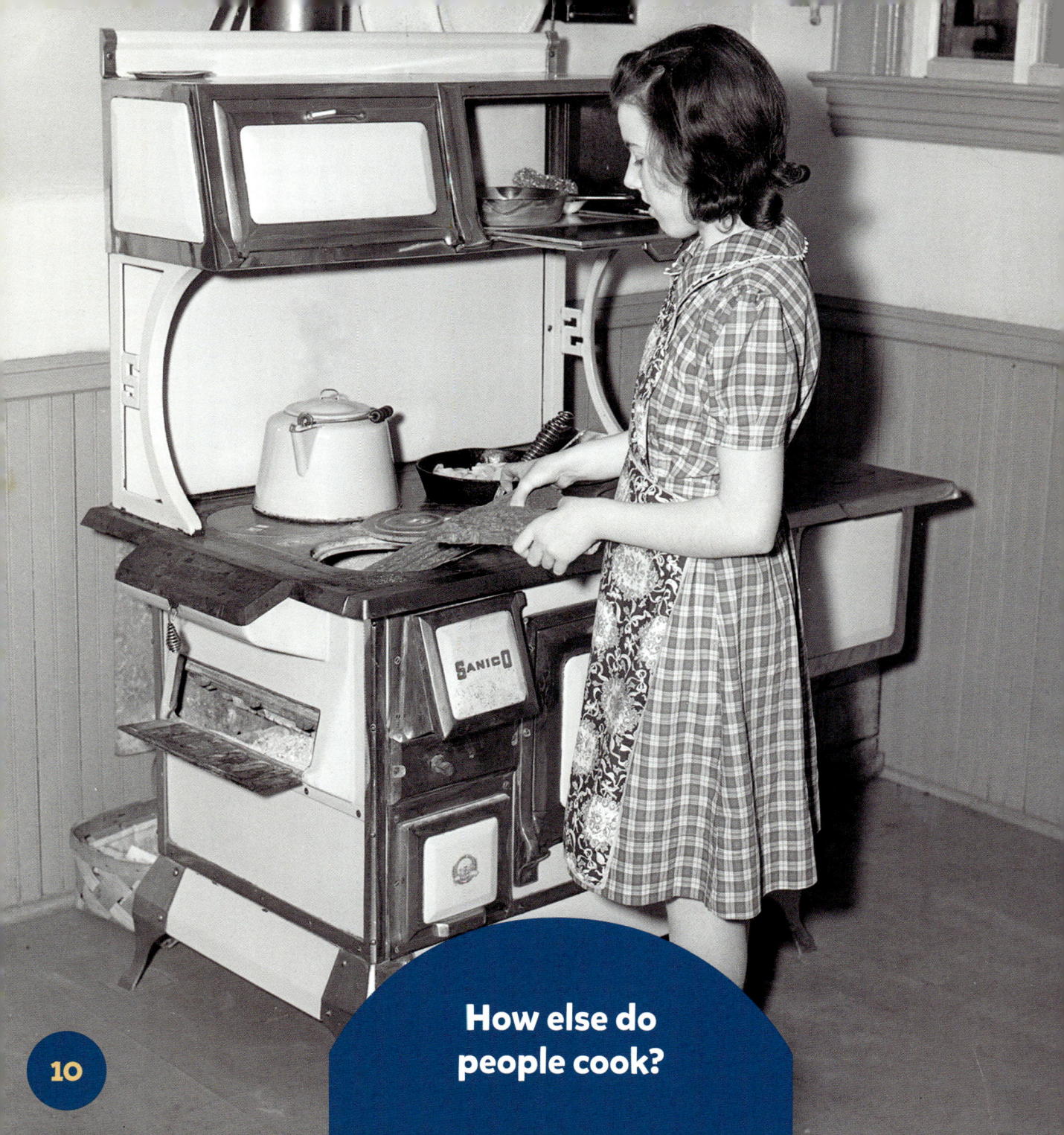

How else do people cook?

THEN
Kitchens had wood stoves.

NOW
We use electric or gas stoves.

THEN
Toilets were outside.

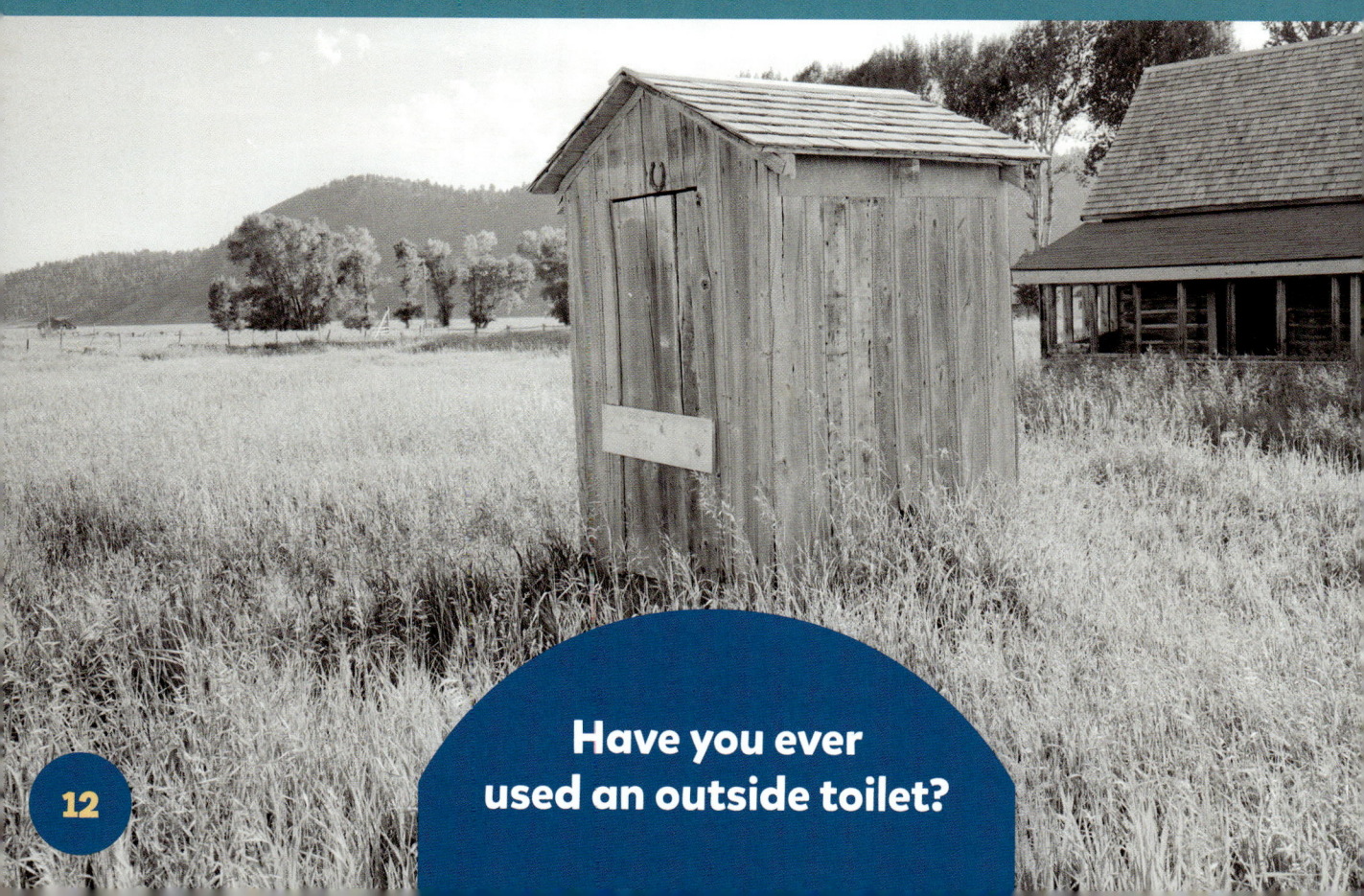

Have you ever used an outside toilet?

NOW

Toilets are inside.

THEN

People used buckets of water to fill tubs.

NOW

Homes have running water.

How do you dry clothes?

THEN
Families washed clothes with boards.

NOW
We wash clothes with electric washers.

THEN
Families used fires to heat their homes.

NOW

Heaters keep homes warm.

Homes today have helpful new tools.

You Connect!

Does your home have any old tools?

How would your life be different without electricity?

How can you learn more about how people lived in the past?

Social and Emotional Snapshot

Student voice is crucial to building reader confidence. Ask the reader:

What is your favorite part of this book?

What is something you learned from this book?

Did this book remind you of any tools in your home?

Opportunities for social and emotional learning are everywhere. How can you connect the topic of this book to the SEL competencies below?

Relationship Skills
Self-Awareness
Social Awareness

Photo Glossary

Learn More

Butterworth, Christine. *How Does My Home Work?* Somerville, MA: Candlewick Press, 2018.

Dinmont, Kerry. *Homes Past and Present.* Minneapolis: Lerner Publications, 2019.

Lawrence, Carol. *Homes: From Then to Now.* Chicago: Albert Whitman & Company, 2021.

Index

clothes, 16, 17

electric, 7, 9, 11, 17

lamps, 7

stoves, 11

toilets, 12, 13

water, 14, 15

Photo Acknowledgments

The images in this book are used with the permission of: © Monkey Business Images/Shutterstock Images, pp. 4–5; © Everett Collection/Shutterstock Images, pp. 6–7, 23 (oil lamp); © Odua Images/Shutterstock Images, p. 7; © Library of Congress, pp. 8, 10, 12, 14, 18; © Lopolo/Shutterstock Images, pp. 9, 23 (fridge); © Image Source Trading Ltd/Shutterstock Images, pp. 11, 23 (stove); © New Africa/Shutterstock Images, pp. 13, 15; © Library of Congress/Wikimedia Commons, p. 16; © wavebreakmedia/Shutterstock Images, pp. 17, 20; © Sergey Malkov/Shutterstock Images, pp. 19, 23 (heater).

Cover Photographs: © dhughes9/iStockphoto (outhouse); © New Africa/Shutterstock Images (toilet)

Design Elements: Mighty Media, Inc.

Copyright © 2024 by Lerner Publishing Group, Inc.

All rights reserved. International copyright secured. No part of this book may be reproduced, stored in a retrieval system, or transmitted in any form or by any means—electronic, mechanical, photocopying, recording, or otherwise—without the prior written permission of Lerner Publishing Group, Inc., except for the inclusion of brief quotations in an acknowledged review.

Lerner Publications Company
An imprint of Lerner Publishing Group, Inc.
241 First Avenue North
Minneapolis, MN 55401 USA

For reading levels and more information, look up this title at www.lernerbooks.com.

Main body text set in Mikado a Medium.
Typeface provided by Hannes von Doehren.

Library of Congress Cataloging-in-Publication Data

Names: Leed, Percy, 1968-author.
Title: Homes : a look at then and now / Percy Leed.
Description: Minneapolis : Lerner Publications, [2024.] | Series: Read about the past. (Read for a better world) | Includes bibliographical references and index. | Audience: Ages 5–8 | Audience: Grades K–1 | Summary: "How did we live in our homes before electricity and running water? Readers will find out in this book about homes then and now, with full-color photographs that bring the past to life"— Provided by publisher.
Identifiers: LCCN 2022033291 (print) | LCCN 2022033292 (ebook) | ISBN 9781728491462 (library binding) | ISBN 9798765603512 (paperback) | ISBN 9781728499383 (ebook)
Subjects: LCSH: Dwellings—History—Juvenile literature.
Classification: LCC GT172 .L44 2023 (print) | LCC GT172 (ebook) | DDC 392.3/6—dc23/eng/20220822

LC record available at https://lccn.loc.gov/2022033291
LC ebook record available at https://lccn.loc.gov/2022033292

Manufactured in the United States of America
1 – CG – 7/15/23